Clarinet/Tenor Sax

How to Use the CD Accompaniment:

A melody cue appears on the right channel only. If your CD player has a balance adjustment, you can adjust the volume of the melody by turning down the right channel.

ISBN 0-7935-8460-4

7777 W. BLUEMOUND RD. P.O. BOX 13819 MILWAUKEE, WI 53213

Visit Hal Leonard Online at
www.halleonard.com

CONTENTS

WE WILL ROCK YOU ◆1
(Recorded by QUEEN)

Words and Music by
BRIAN MAY

Clarinet/Tenor Sax

Heavy Rock

WILD THING ◆2
(Recorded by THE TROGGS)

Words and Music by
CHIP TAYLOR

Clarinet/Tenor Sax

Lower notes optional

DANGER ZONE ◆3

(from the Motion Picture TOP GUN)

Words and Music by
GIORGIO MORODER and TOM WHITLOCK

Clarinet/Tenor Sax

ROCK & ROLL-PART II ◆4
(The Hey Song)

Words and Music by
GARY GLITTER and MIKE LEANDER

Clarinet/Tenor Sax

TWIST AND SHOUT ◆5

(Recorded by THE BEATLES)

Clarinet/Tenor Sax

Words and Music by
BERT RUSSELL and PHIL MEDLEY

BORN TO BE WILD ◆6

(Recorded by STEPPENWOLF)

Words and Music by
MARS BONFIRE

Clarinet/Tenor Sax

FINAL COUNTDOWN ◆7◆

Clarinet/Tenor Sax

Words and Music by
JOEY TEMPEST

I GOT YOU 🔶8

(I Feel Good)

Clarinet/Tenor Sax

Words and Music by
JAMES BROWN

DEVIL WITH THE BLUE DRESS 9

Clarinet/Tenor Sax

Words and Music by
WILLIAM STEVENSON and FREDERICK LONG

Pumpin' Rock

GONNA MAKE YOU SWEAT
(Everybody Dance Now)

Words and Music by
ROBERT CLIVILLES and FREDERICK B. WILLIAMS

Clarinet/Tenor Sax

Y.M.C.A. ◆11

(Recorded by THE VILLAGE PEOPLE)

Words and Music by JACQUES MORALI,
HENRI BELOLO and VICTOR WILLIS

Clarinet/Tenor Sax

GET READY FOR THIS 12

(Recorded by 2 UNLIMITED)

Clarinet/Tenor Sax

By JEAN PAUL DE COSTER, FILIP DE WILDE and SIMON HARRIS

© Copyright 1992 by DECOS PUBLISHING and CMINOR MUSIC o/b/o MUSIC OF LIFE
All Rights for DECOS PUBLISHING in the United States and Canada Controlled and Administered by MUSIC CORPORATION OF AMERICA, INC.
All Rights for CMINOR MUSIC o/b/o MUSIC OF LIFE Administered by COPYRIGHT MANAGEMENT, INC.
International Copyright Secured All Rights Reserved
MCA music publishing

PLAY MORE OF YOUR FAVORITE SONGS
WITH GREAT INSTRUMENTAL FOLIOS FROM HAL LEONARD

Best of the Beatles
89 of the greatest songs from the legends of Liverpool, including: All You Need Is Love • And I Love Her • The Fool on the Hill • Got to Get You into My Life • Here, There, and Everywhere • Let It Be • Norwegian Wood • Something • Ticket to Ride • and more.

00847217	Flute	$9.95
00847218	Clarinet	$9.95
00847219	Alto Sax	$9.95
00847220	Trumpet	$9.95
00847221	Trombone	$9.95

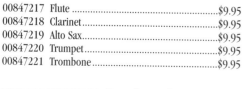

Broadway Showstoppers
47 incredible selections from over 25 shows. Songs include: All I Ask of You • Cabaret • Camelot • Climb Ev'ry Mountain • Comedy Tonight • Don't Cry for Me Argentina • Hello, Dolly! • I Dreamed a Dream • Maria • Memory • Oklahoma! • Seventy-Six Trombones • and many more!

08721339	Flute	$6.95
08721340	Bb Clarinet	$6.95
08721341	Eb Alto Sax	$6.95
08721342	Bb Trumpet/Bb Tenor Sax	$6.95
08721343	Trombone (Bass Clef Instruments)	$6.95

Choice Jazz Standards
30 songs, including: All the Things You Are • A Foggy Day • The Girl From Ipanema • Just in Time • My Funny Valentine • Quiet Nights of Quiet Stars • Smoke Gets in Your Eyes • Watch What Happens • and many more.

00850276	Flute	$5.95
00850275	Clarinet	$5.95
00850274	Alto Sax	$5.95
00850273	Trumpet	$5.95
00850272	Trombone	$5.95

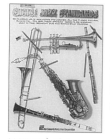

Classic Rock & Roll
31 songs, including: Blue Suede Shoes • Blueberry Hill • Dream Lover • I Want to Hold Your Hand • The Shoop Shoop Song • Surfin' U.S.A. • and many others.

00850248	Flute	$5.95
00850249	Clarinet	$5.95
00850250	Alto Sax	$5.95
00850251	Trumpet	$5.95
00850252	Trombone	$5.95

The Definitive Jazz Collection
88 songs, including: Ain't Misbehavin' • All the Things You Are • Birdland • Body and Soul • A Foggy Day • Girl From Ipanema • Love for Sale • Mercy, Mercy, Mercy • Moonlight in Vermont • Night and Day • Skylark • Stormy Weather • and more.

08721673	Flute	$9.95
08721674	Clarinet	$9.95
08721675	Alto Sax	$9.95
08721676	Trumpet	$9.95
08721677	Trombone	$9.95

Latin Gold
16 Latin favorites, including: Bésame Mucho • Brazil • Evil Ways • The Girl from Ipanema • Granada • Malaguena • Mas Que Nada • One Note Samba • Perfidia • Quiet Nights of Quiet Stars (Corcovado) • Sama De Orfeu • So Nice (Summer Samba) • Tico Tico • and more.

00841461	Flute	$5.95
00841462	Clarinet	$5.95
00841463	Alto Sax	$5.95
00841464	Tenor Sax	$5.95
00841465	Trumpet	$5.95
00841466	French Horn	$5.95
00841467	Trombone	$5.95

Disney's The Lion King
5 fun solos for students from Disney's blockbuster. Includes: Can You Feel the Love Tonight • Circle of Life • Hakuna Matata • I Just Can't Wait to Be King • Be Prepared.

00849949	Flute	$5.95
00849950	Clarinet	$5.95
00849951	Alto Sax	$5.95
00849952	Trumpet	$5.95
00849953	Trombone	$5.95
00849003	Easy Violin	$5.95
00849004	Viola	$5.95
00849005	Cello	$5.95
00849955	Piano Accompaniment	$10.95

Best of Andrew Lloyd Webber
26 of his best, including: All I Ask of You • Close Every Door • Don't Cry for Me Argentina • I Don't Know How to Love Him • Love Changes Everything • Memory • and more.

00849939	Flute	$6.95
00849940	Clarinet	$6.95
00849941	Trumpet	$6.95
00849942	Alto Sax	$6.95
00849943	Trombone	$6.95
00849015	Violin	$6.95

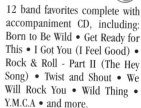

0400